IMAGES OF ENGLAND

FAIRFORD

IMAGES OF ENGLAND

FAIRFORD

JUNE LEWIS-JONES

TEMPUS

Frontispiece: A bird's-eye view of Fairford looking south-west, taken from the church tower in 1978, showing the curve of the ancient thoroughfare (now the A417) as it crosses the River Coln.

First published 2007

Tempus Publishing
Cirencester Road, Chalford,
Stroud, Gloucestershire, GL6 8PE
www.tempus-publishing.com

Tempus Publishing is an imprint of NPI Media Group

British Library Cataloguing in Publication Data.
A catalogue record for this book is available from the British Library.

ISBN 978 0 7524 4475 8

Typesetting and origination by NPI Media Group
Printed in Great Britain

Contents

Acknowledgements

I am grateful to the following people who have given me photographs for my collection that I have used here, or have lent their precious ones to be used specifically in this book.

Mary Vizor p36(T), p41(B), p72 and 40(B)

Terry Butler p37(BR)

Margaret Brown p50

The late Sidney Perry p16(B), p54(TR)

Mark Cowley p56(T)

Jake Sutton p60(T)

Hilary Hainsworth p62(T), p64(T)

Hilda Simpson p65(B)

Stella Nash p66(M)

Shelagh Diplock p73(B)

Alison Hobson p76(B), p108(B), p109(T and B)

Barbara Cheales p81(T)

Jill Cutler p87(B) and p88(T)

Anthony Little p91, p92

MCC Trent Bridge p101(M)

Rosemary Gwynne-Jones p116

Heather Shuttlewood p117(T)

David Mundy p117(B) and p118

Phyllis Glavor p115(B) and Richard Briley for all their help in getting Wally's photo for the book

RIAT p122

Church Missionary Society p124(BL)

Chief Ed Anderson, Fairford Reservation, Manitoba p125(R)

Introduction

What's in a name? How often we consider that well-worn Shakespearian question and more often than not it proves difficult to answer in as few words, simply because the name will have different connotations and meanings to different people. But it is a fact that the mere mention of a name will conjure up an instant image in our mind, and particularly so with a place. It may be a favourite view or a building that has some personal significance, therefore it is generally by association that we have a feeling for a place and particularly for its people.

The advent of photography in mid-Victorian times and the advanced technology since has given us the means by which an instant can be captured as a visual image to be kept and viewed at will – that is, of course, providing that there is someone with a camera to record it at the time! Often, of course, it was the special occasion for which the photograph was set up or posed that has been preserved in family albums, but it is the chance shot of the commonplace that is more interesting in the placing of a place and its people in context of their time.

These images of Fairford aim to create a visual outline of its history over the last 100 years or so and, equally important, to give a picture of the town as it is today because we are, after all, making history every day in one way or another. It is interesting to have a reminder of how national change has been reflected at local level and how, even in our erstwhile quiet and rural corner of Britain the world has not passed us by. There are inevitably gaps for which no photographic records exist: the war years, for instance, are particularly difficult; mainly because very few families owned cameras at that time and films were almost impossible to obtain, any photographs that were taken would have been personal ones of the family and strict security regulations prohibited the taking of any military activities.

Clambering up the torturous spiralling steps of the church tower to get a bird's-eye view looking down on the town, and a close appreciation of the intricate stone work that Peter Juggins wrought on the exquisite stone pinnacles that we normally only see by looking up from the ground, is one of my outstanding memories locked into the photographs. Likewise, my research over many decades into the history of my home town led me to visit 'that other Fairford' to which, due to limited space, I can give but a brief visual glimpse in this book.

Those who met the contingent of the Ojibwa Fairford Indians when they returned my visit (twenty-six fold!) to commemorate the 500th anniversary of the consecration of our St Mary's church will have their own memories, too.

I hope that this collection will enable the reader to share vicariously in the myriad happenings and events and everyday life of Fairford and its people, because it is the people that make the place what it has become and is today. So for whatever reason you have this book in your hand, because it bears the name Fairford – whether as a visitor to see a little more behind the scenes, or to evoke memories of a past association or, for those of us who are fortunate enough to call it home – I dedicate this book to Fairfordians, past and present and, especially, to my husband, Ralph.

Welcome to Fairford - entering the town from the west.

one

The Town

Instantly Fairford – the old mill with St Mary's church in view.

Another well-loved spot – the naturalised lake formed from a disused gravel pit close by the Coln at the far east of the parish which Fairfordians are fighting to save from extensive development.

The flood waters in the mill meadow in the year 2000 followed the course of the ancient ford from which Fairford got its name in Saxon times, *Fagranforda* – meaning 'fair' (easy to cross) ford.

The town bridge in the 1890s showing the river coming up to the road edge. This allowed horse-drawn wagons to be driven into the shallow water to swell the wooden spokes when getting loose in the rim.

Fairford gained its status as a market town when it was granted a charter from Henry I who held the manor under the Crown. This ram lamb wears a collecting box for the Red Cross in 1914. Fred Cole of Milton Farm is sitting on the left.

The old livestock market lapsed at the outset of the Second World War, but was re-opened as a general weekly market in 1986.

The splendid seventeenth-century mansion in the Park, designed by Valentine Strong for the Barker family who held the manor until it was purchased by the Ernest Cook Trust in 1945. The house fell into disrepair after being requisitioned for military use during the Second World War, and was demolished in 1955. Farmor's School was built on the site.

Above left: The obelisk, a feature of the eighteenth-century landscaping, marked the northernmost vista of the manor.

Above right: The classical 'temple' from Fairford Park is now at Barnsley House, home of the late Rosemary Verey, celebrated garden expert and writer.

Park Street, formerly known as Calcott Street, borders the south side of Fairford Park.

The old gamekeeper's cottage in Park Street was moved back from the street edge in Victorian times; the brothers Brown, local builders, buried a bottle in the foundations containing their name and date of the rebuilding.

Morgan Hall, an Elizabethan house, where Captain Morgan's Roundheads camped on their way to Cirencester in the Civil War. It was later the Dower House of the manor.

East End House, another fine Georgian building.

London Street, the general plan of which has altered little over the last century, except for the heavy flow of traffic taking the place of the lone horse-drawn cart.

Victorian Christmas meat show outside Perry's family butchers in London Street.

The Bull Hotel, which originated as a medieval wool merchants' hall, flanks the whole west side of the Market Place.

Above left: The Big Alley leading from the High Street to the Croft embodies the town's country market past.

Above right: Cotswold dry stone walls, built in the same way as the Romans did, are one of the outstanding features throughout the town.

The only major change in the mainly eighteenth-century High Street was the rebuilding of the house and shop (marked with crosses) as the post office and Lloyds Bank in 1901.

The Little Alley to the left of the former post-office doorway also leads to the Croft.

The top of the High Street in 1955.

A traffic jam of a different kind at the bottom of the High Street in the snows of 1963.

The Police Station built in 1860 in the High Street is now a private house. A new Police Station was built in 2002 in London Street.

The old White Hart Inn at the bottom of the Market Place undergoing conversion to cottages in 1988, an historical turn around as the inn originated as a row of cottages built for the masons working on the church in the fifteenth century.

This small open-fronted building at the end of the White Hart housed the old horse-drawn fire engine as shown in this picture of 1958.

The removal of the fire engine house allowed access to build new houses at White Hart Court.

This ancient row of cottages at East End, scheduled for demolition to make way for a new development, spearheaded the move to form Fairford Preservation Society.

Derelict cottages alongside Gables Cottages were demolished for the new Beaumoor and Keble Lawns development.

East End cottages reflect a variety of building styles as shown here in the 1940s.

Pear Tree Cottage dating back to around 1700, a former yeoman's house, lost some 2 acres of land to development in the 1950s.

Milton Street, looking towards the town bridge, snowbound in 1963.

Milton Street, from the town bridge, in the Millennium floods. Thomas Witchell wrote these lines in 1925 of a similar flooding:

> *Thinks I, Fairford is rightly named,*
> *It's really now a fair ford.*
> *The Bull Tap, too, was also blocked,*
> *No one could go therein,*
> *And likewise in the White Hart yard,*
> *'Twas flowing much within.*

The west end of Milton Street, *c.* 1910.

Milton Street crossroads, cornered by Coln House School (formerly The Retreat Asylum) on the left, with the Marlborough Arms cornering Coronation Street, alongside Old Tracey, dating back to the early 1600s, on the right. The small green, once much larger than now, was where the old drovers rested their sheep and cattle before moving on to market.

The Virgills, Horcott, showing how the backs of the cottages faced the road.

The same row of cottages after Yells Brothers, local builders, turned them 'face about'.

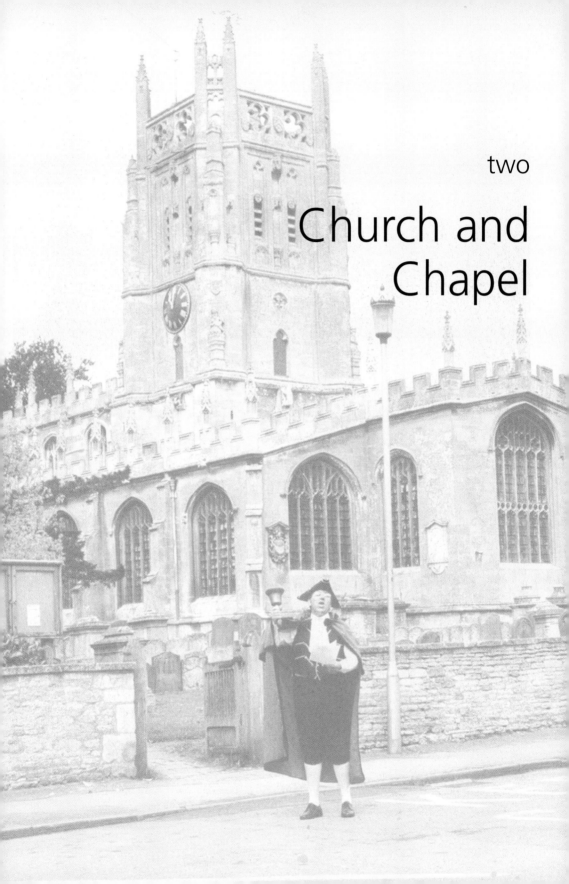

two

Church and
Chapel

Above: Horcott Road, date unknown, captured by J.W. Gardner, who had a photographic studio in Fairford in the early 1900s.

Left: St Mary's church, rebuilt in the fifteenth century by John Tame, a wealthy wool merchant, is famous for its complete set of medieval stained-glass windows depicting the story of the Bible. Maurice Jones cries the news of local events in the tradition traced back to the early eighteenth century, wearing a costume based on that period.

Right: Stephen Yells and Mark Cowley set off on a sponsored ride for the Historic Churches Trust funds, watched by the verger, Sid Jacques.

Below: The bells of St Mary's awaiting collection for recasting in 1927.

Above left: Bill Godwin, tower captain for many years, literally teaching the ropes to his daughter Susan.

Above right: A team of scientists measured the sound effects on the medieval windows just prior to the arrival of Concorde to RAF Fairford Base. It was discovered that the supersonic boom from the aircraft would not have such an adverse effect on the glass as would holding down the lowest note of the church organ for a prolonged period!

Above left: Peter Juggins, the stone mason who carved the complete set of pinnacles that had been destroyed in the freak whirlwind of 1971.

Above right: Dorothy Paton, former mayor of Fairford, who spearheaded the mammoth project of producing a complete set of tapestry kneelers, choir seat cushions and a full complement of ecclesiastical robes and altar furnishings in time for the church's 500th anniversary in 1997.

The cannonball mark on the wall of the south porch is a reminder of the Civil War. The small headstone bears the date 1668, but the larger one to William Beenham, a master of Farmor's School is somewhat a mystery as, according to the memoirs of John Woolley, a successful printer, the grave is that of his father, also named John Woolley, a gardener at Morgan Hall who died in 1833.

Tiddles Two pauses in 2007 in front of the tomb of Tiddles, church cat 1963-1980, who is buried in a prestigious spot facing the south entrance.

The nave facing east.

The experimental arrangement with the clearance of the front pews allowing for a small altar in the nave and scope for a wider range of activities.

Keble House, birthplace of John Keble, founder of the famous Oxford Movement. It was called Court Close in Victorian times when it was home to the Doctors Cornwall, who held their surgeries there.

The Vicarage for many years, the house on the extreme left of this view of London Street about 1930 later became the Hyperion Hotel, with a betting shop, now a nursing home.

A new Vicarage in the process of being built in the Croft in 1957.

The Congregational chapel, built in the Croft in 1862, in the process of being demolished in 1966. During the period when it was no longer in use as a chapel it accommodated many local activities including youth and drama groups, Home Guards, rummage sales and as a dining hall for school dinners.

Now the United church for the Nonconformist bodies, the Baptist chapel in Milton Street was built in 1853.

The Roman Catholic church of St Thomas of Canterbury, built at Horcott in 1845 reputedly out of a bequest by Lady de Mauley of Hatherop Castle but with no resident priest. Application was made in 1844 for the holding of regular services and the conducting of marriages. A number of the Polish families settled at the Park Camp after the war are buried in the churchyard. Relatives leave lighted candles in decorated holders to burn all night on the graves at All Souls' and All Saints' Days.

three

Transport

The schoolchildren were given time off from lessons to see the first car come through Fairford. Dr Charles Bloxsome was the first man in the town to own a motor car. Here, he is in his 1905 steam-driven 'Locomobile'.

John Faulkner's latest car was also an object of interest when he came to preside as magistrate at the Petty Sessions court.

Charles Morse came to Fairford with the opening of the railway in 1873 and was presented with a mantel clock at a ceremony at The Bull on his retirement.

Above left: His son, Bill Morse, on his retirement as engine driver on the London–Cardiff run, came to Fairford as signalman.

Above right: Mary Law was the first lady guard to be appointed on the Fairford–Oxford GWR line.

Ted Law, extreme left, was a 'top link' driver at Fairford and served on the railway for forty-five years until the line was closed.

The old Fairford Flyer had an overall speed restriction of 50 mph and its twenty-one mile journey to Oxford took one hour and eleven minutes, with stops at ten stations.

Despite strong local opposition, Fairford railway was closed. This is the last train to run from the station on 18 June 1962. The bridge that spanned the track was demolished soon after.

A trio of wheels for the brothers Peyman around 1900: W.H. with his boneshaker, Charles with his Penny-farthing and John with a 'modern bike'.

William Westbury, who worked at Park Farm, driving a traction engine around 1910.

Nancy and Doddy Thornton in their triple donkey cart at Fairford House.

Half a century later the Thornton sisters took to a tricycle made for two.

Beryl and Gwynneth Edmonds try their hand at a three-wheeler Bath chair at Croft House.

Bikes and trikes, decorated in carnival mode, were always a popular class, as this group shows in 1925.

Above left: Charlie and Annie Gosling setting off for a Sunday ride out in 1898.

Above right: Fred Keylock took to a tricycle on his retirement as chauffeur-mechanic to Dr Bloxsome.

Busby and Townsend's Garage, the showroom that stood close to the town bridge in Milton Street was formerly that of Constable's the coach maker.

Marion Wall, June Mead and Mary Evans serving petrol at Busby's Garage in 1955.

The extent of Busby's Garage, with its forecourt pumps, shop and workshops can be seen in the bird's eye view of Milton Street taken from the church tower. New houses now fill the site, with only the small stone-built reception office remaining alongside the house – an attractive corner as Fairford Flowers.

four

Hotels and Inns

Above: The Bull Hotel has been a forum for much of the town's business over the centuries since medieval times when the flourishing wool trade was centred here. Overseers of the Poor met there to decide upon charity rates; the protracted meetings of the Thames & Severn Canal Commissioners and even lengthier ones on the railway; inquests, magistrates' court hearings and the County of Gloucester banking services were all accommodated in turn, with market dinners, celebration balls and smoking concerts adding to the social scene. As a posting house it had few equals – the London coach called three times a week in 1792 when there was stabling for thirty horses, which were taken through the front wooden doors, as shown here, along a central cobbled passage. The Reading Room for the townsfolk was in the part on the left with the bay front. On the opening of the railway, a regular carriage and carrier service was operated from the hotel to convey the passengers and their luggage as in this picture taken about 1908.

Below: The Bull Tap literally had its beer supply 'on tap' from a pipe running under the road from The Bull Hotel – thus saving the landlord paying for a second licence! The Bull was generally used by farmers and tradesmen, while the workmen and labourers felt more comfortable in the cosy cottage-like Tap, which closed in 1957.

This sketch of 1804 of the Market Place shows the sign of The Swan on the extreme right, facing The Bull. The Swan was opened by 1610 and served the Gloucester coaches for over 150 years. It later became R.W. Bridges Grocers shop (now the Co-op Village Store). An even earlier inn, called The Cross Keys, was rebuilt as a private house about 1790 – probably as Montague House, opposite the church.

The Three Magpies has been closed as a pub for many decades now. Standing in isolation on the Cirencester Road at the west edge of the parish, it was a favourite meeting place for the VWH Hunt and a strategic point to which the Home Guards marched on their training sessions.

Two hostlers were recorded in 1327 and 'an inn' in 1419. In 1905 Fairford had a total of sixteen alehouses, twenty-two beer houses and three off-licenses – a proportion of one licensed house to 127 inhabitants and catering for an increase in road and rail travellers as reflected in the name of the Railway Inn, shown here with John Kibblewhite, the landlord in his pony and trap.

Despite the railway closing, the Railway Inn is still a busy pub with only an addition to the front entrance and the mode of transport making any real difference to the scene ninety years later. The entrance to the East Glos Engineering works, which has served the agricultural community for over a century, is to be seen on the extreme left of the picture.

The Eight Bells on the corner of East End takes its name from the peal of eight bells of St Mary's church.

The Plough in London Street has Tudor cottage neighbours to one side and the Palmer Hall on the other.

The George, like the adjoining Bull Hotel, of which it is now part – except for the former bar area which is the current post office – were faced with plaster as in this picture of about 1910.

With its Tudor half-timbered framework revealed, the George stands as an architectural heritage piece on the corner of the Market Place. The White Hart sign can be clearly seen on the left of the former ancient inn, with The Bull Tap in the far distance as the road curves round to the town bridge. The Cotswold Grill café on the extreme left became Leo's restaurant and is now Allium.

A highlight of the year for the George regulars was the annual coach trip to the seaside, organised by Sid Hope the landlord.

The Marlborough Arms, once regarded as the drovers' pub, who stopped here on their way to market, corners Coronation Street and Cirencester Road.

Cheers! This could have been taken in any of the hostelries in the 1930s, but was probably set up in the studio of Charlie Powell who was the official town photographer.

The picturesque pub, which served locals for generations and was much loved by the American servicemen as it was just down the hill from the airbase, is now no more than a memory. Closed by 1990, there is no trace of its ever being; new houses now stand on the site.

The longest serving landlord and lady of The Carriers Arms at Horcott, Derek and Kath Jones embody the very essence of an English country pub – with good ale and good cheer.

five

Shops, Trades and Farms

Mr Burge at his saddlers and fly-fishing tackle shop that stood in the entrance through to Back Lane.

Mr Hayes who took over the trade, left of the doorway with his son, Herbie with a horse's collar on his shoulder, and 'Spinney' Cooper taken in 1914.

With so many farms in the area there was always a demand for harness – note the nosebag on the horse here with Kath Geach from Milton Farm.

Electrifying the river by the town bridge to catch eels to protect the fishing trade operated from The Bull in 1959.

Another legacy of a bygone trade is the splendid range of iron railings on the Mill Bridge, wrought at Edgar Buxton Chew's Waterloo Lane forge in 1862.

Above left: Inside the family grocers of R.W. Bridges in the early 1930s.

Above right: Leonard and Sidney Perry outside their butcher's shop in London Street – a family business that served Fairford for about a century. Note the traditional glazed tiled base of the window.

W. Law's 'wireless shop' at the bottom end of the Market Place, decorated for a carnival weekend in the mid-1920s, by which time the term 'radio' was the modern term and electrical supplies were more in demand. The shop became Leo's Restaurant and is now Allium which has recently featured in a television programme on award-winning chefs using locally produced food.

Yells Brothers, an established family firm since 1858, have left their imprint on much of the town's buildings, including the Palmer Hall, the rear extension (formerly the verandahs) at the Cottage Hospital and as here.

At the Lodge House of Burdocks.

The ladies of the Nash family pose for a picture in 1904 at the gas works that were started in 1852 when John Nash (reputed to have fathered twenty-one children) came as manager to Fairford Gas & Coke Co. in Back Lane. Gas was made here (note the retorts in the background) until 1936 when it was made at Swindon but still stored at Fairford until the town's conversion to North Sea Gas in 1972.

Not only has the gas lamp disappeared, the grass triangle on which it stood with the three-fingered signpost has now been replaced by a traffic bollard in front of Park Villas.

F.R. Stevens' cycle shop at the foot of The Bull alley later became the post office and now The Bridge Restaurant.

Alessandro and Lucianna D'Elia bring the colour and flavour of their ancestral Italian cuisine to The Bridge Restaurant, following in the traditional footsteps of their father, Leo, who ran his restaurant on the corner of the Market Place for a great number of years.

Three generations of family bakers: Mr Raven on his rounds by pony cart.

Bill Radway (Mr Raven's son-in-law) with his famous Fairford lardy cakes in 1977.

Derek Radway, using the same long-handled wooden peel as his father and grandfather to remove the loaf tins from the 100-year-old ovens.

The end of an era of home-baked bread and cakes: Vera Miles, right, serves the last customers.

Radways Bakery reverted to three cottages in the new millennium. Park Corner Pharmacy has now moved to the middle of the High Street. The Misses Iles ran a small private girls' school in the house before the Manning family opened up their chemist's shop around the 1890s.

Baldwin hardware and ironmongery shop with the plastered front in 1915. Mr and Mrs Baldwin are standing in the doorway, with sons, Horace to the left, George and Ray in the entrance of the Big Alley. Note the range of tools, cans, chests and tin ware displayed. J.C. Peyman & Sons continued the business until the turn of this century, by which time the stonework was revealed.

The vibrant and evocative paintings of the highly acclaimed artist, Jake Sutton, now bring zing and zest in line and colour to the High Street in the Kim Sutton Gallery.

A few other trades and shops advertising in 1939.

C. Edmonds & Son had a comprehensive department store in the centre of the High Street, with an additional furniture shop and ladies' hairdressing salon (under the name of Peggie Powell) at the bottom end of the Market Place; both shops are shown here as they were closing down.

The old Edmonds' front windows became dressed as H.M. Powell, Draper, Clothier and Tailor for the filming by the BBC of *Wreath of Roses* in 1986.

Artistic licence was taken further for the film set as A.E. Powell, Stationer and Drug Store since Victorian times, as shown here in 1948.

When the shop was recast in H.M. Powell's Draper shop next to the Little Alley and Lloyds Bank!

To confuse the locals even more there was Fulton Mackay nibbling into a toffee apple at a fairground set up in the Mill meadow.

Cyril and Meg Norman at Horcott Farm in the 1940s with, left to right: Ron, May, Iris (on gate) Wallie (on gate) and Margaret.

Park Farm dairyman, Charlie Westbury, in the 1930s.

The tradition of horse-drawn milk deliveries ended in the late 1970s with Audrey Cowley, Fairford's 'milk lady' for seventeen years.

Oh! to be a farmer's boy – Arthur Simpson as a boy driving a tractor in pre-war days.

Milton Farm at the top of Mill Lane is still very much a working farm. The house was built as a twin to Park Farm, with identical proportions and imposing frontage, in the 1850s. Waiten Hill Farmhouse (on the opposite side of the Mill Lane) was also built by the Barker family to a similar plan, on a slightly smaller scale, in 1893. Tom Paton, pictured here with his wife Susie, and family, follows in his father Andrew's farming footsteps.

Tom Rymer of Waiten Hill Farm who bred the prize beast for the Coronation ox roast of 1937, with Arthur Woodward the butcher to his left and Mr Hayward, stockman, wearing smart breeches and gaiters on his right, attracting an interested crowd outside The Bull Hotel.

The long barn of Cotswold stone in the redundant farm yard at East End where Briggs & Rickards, agricultural engineers, kept their fleet of steam and traction engines for contract hire – later used by Barrett & Cuss agricultural contractors. The barn was saved from demolition and forms part of the housing development at Keble Lawns.

Shep Jones and family pose for the camera at sheep-shearing time.

Moor Farm terminates the ancient tithing of East End – the old farmhouse dates back in part some 400 years.

No longer a working farm, although the fields are still cultivated, Beaumoor Farm (as it was anciently named) barns and outbuildings have been converted to houses. Here, Shirley Curtis makes her tracks delivering the Christmas post as she had for eighteen years.

Park Farm House, built by the Barker family in the mid-nineteenth century reflects the grander scale home to attract the 'gentleman farmer' complimentary to a manorial estate. Here, the Iles family pose in suitable style in 1909. Three generations of the Iles family ran the farm in Park Street before it was closed down and the house was sold. A large stone barn in the yard was demolished to make way for a small housing development, but the Tudor wool store was converted with the stable block into what is now Glebe Court House.

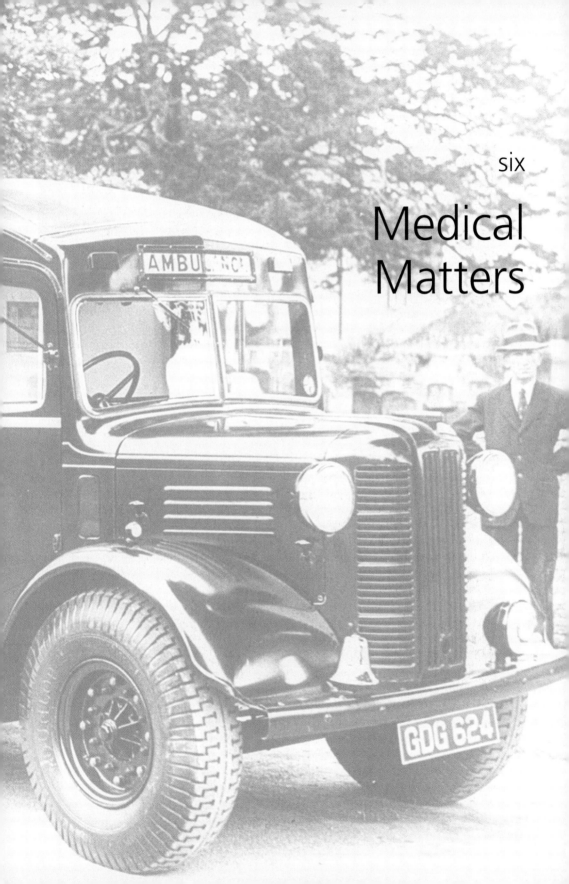

six

Medical
Matters

One of the earliest cottage hospitals in England, Fairford's Rural Hospital was opened in Park Street in the block of four cottages at the end of the eighteenth-century row (indicated by the arrow) in 1867.

Laying the foundation stone of the new Cottage Hospital in the Croft in 1887 on land given by J.R. Raymond Barker, Lord of the Manor, on the site of the old Workhouse. Some 105,000 red bricks, all made locally at Mr Dunn's brickworks at Waiten Hill were used by Mr Baldwin, local builder, to build the eight-bed hospital, which included a small operating theatre, at a total cost of £1,357 – all paid for by public subscription through donations and collections and fund-raising.

A new small ward and a bedroom for a nursing sister were added in 1900, paid for by the Gibbs family of Ablington Manor, in memory of their son, J. Arthur Gibbs, author of the country classic *A Cotswold Village*. The cost that year for 'food of all kinds' was 10d a day per patient, plus a halfpenny a day each for wine or spirits which included the nursing staff!

The back garden about 1910.

Croft House where Dr Charles Bloxsome ran his surgery from 1903 to be followed by his son Dr Harold Bloxsome until 1950 when Dr Charlton Shaw took over the practice, to be joined by Dr Michael Veale in 1951.

The Bloxsome family at the back of Croft House with Dr Charles Bloxsome and his son, Harold (seen here as a young lad with Myra the dog on his knee, sitting in front of his father).

Drs Shaw and Veale served the practice for over thirty years in Hilary Cottage, the former Ebenezer Chapel in Coronation Street, and the name has been carried on to the new, first purpose-built surgery in the town's long history.

The imposing Georgian spread of what became The Retreat Asylum shows the original house of 1822 cornering Milton Street at the old Turnpike road leading to Horcott, built by Alexander Iles who was granted a licence for 'a Mad House to keep any number of lunatics not exceeding ten'. An extension was built to the left of the main house in 1823 to accommodate up to twenty-four patients, segregating male from female and first from second class, i.e. paupers. Further building over part of the extensive gardens became necessary as the number of patients increased. By 1837 there were some 140 in 'The House' from various social backgrounds and from as far away as Shropshire; of that number only twenty-one were registered as 'private patients'.

Nurses enjoying a break in the summer house at the back of The Retreat.

Nurse Davis, the district nurse, founded her Baby Clinic in 1914. She is seen here (second from left at the back) at a clinic Christmas party in 1931.

Fairford had its first ambulance in 1930, purchased for £57 9s 8d, 'due to the generosity of Sir William Morris'. This one was bought by local donations in 1934 at a cost of £267. Busby's Garage maintained it and supplied the drivers. Arthur Bailey can be seen on the right. The League of Friends has bought successive ambulances since its formation in 1970.

All the beds were eventually replaced by modern Kingsfund type. This bed was donated by Fairford Steam Rally, represented by Rosemary Yells (fourth from left). Also present: Sister Jenny Tudor with Laurie Carey, June Lewis and Gerry Beames, founder members of the League of Friends. Charlie Jones is the real 'model' patient.

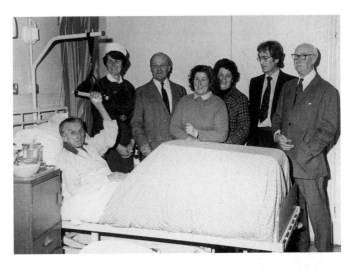

Television personality, Anneka Rice, under the watchful eye of Sister Margaret Shaw and the local press, officially opened the new Day Room, financed by the League in 1997.

Sunshine and smiles from staff and patients in the garden at the back of the hospital in 2003.

Tears and tributes at the Valediction Service at the front door as it closed to in-patient care after 119 years on 1 March 2006.

seven

Schools

Left: Elizabeth Farmor (detail from an oil painting) who left a considerable legacy and specific instructions for 'the Benefit of a Free School to be taught within the parish of Fairford'. She was the granddaughter of Andrew Barker, Lord of the Manor, and died unmarried in 1705.

Below: After a lengthy delay, the case and cause of which were finally settled in the Court of Chancery, Fairford Free School with master's house, complete with brewery, was built for £543 8s and opened its doors to the first pupils on Friday 24 November 1738 for, 'sixty poor boys of the parish' between the ages of five and twelve years. The two-storey extension at the back was added in 1815 as a girls' school, but was run separately (under its own headmistress) from the boys' school until 1922 when the school became co-educational under Mr Hedges and was renamed Farmor's School after its chief benefactor.

After Farmor's had become the secondary school for the area of some dozen villages and outgrown its original home, the building re-opened as Fairford Centre on 24 February 1979 as the town's Jubilee project. In a poor state of disrepair, the old school was bought jointly by the Town Council and St Mary's church council celebrated by an official opening in 2002 by June Lewis-Jones attended by that year's festival queen and attendants and (left to right): Lynn Phillips, Roger Phillips, Jenny Collyer, Len Eales, Trevor Hing, Chris Roberts, Tim Mowat, Quentin Tailford and Alan Baker. With a substantial grant from the Heritage Lottery Fund, the old school is currently being extensively repaired and refurbished to meet the needs of the twenty-first century as Fairford Community and Heritage Centre.

The earliest known photograph of Fairford Boys' School, April 1879. George Orpin was headmaster with 100 boys on roll.

John Taylor with his class of prize-winning young gardeners in 1907, two years after the school had its own garden at West End. Mr Taylor (who later married Miss Hartwell, headmistress of the girls' school) served as head teacher for over thirty-eight years.

Infants and Farmor's schoolchildren joined together to celebrate Empire Day in 1908.

The first cookery lessons were taught by Mrs Nora Cheales (wife of the vicar of Hatherop) in 1920 in Milton Hall (now the Vortex) which was used variously as a showroom for Constable's horseless carriages, elections and teetotallers' lectures – next door to the Marlborough Arms pub!

A cookery class prepares for a pancake race down the High Street in 1958.

Above left: A classroom tea party in the 1950s, supervised by Glyn Morgan, geography and woodwork teacher.

Above right: Mr Hedges' ninety-ninth birthday was celebrated (a few months before he died) with his old pupils, Peter Egerton, Daphne Webb, Edna Jefferies and Les Radway, and many generations of younger ones under the headship of Chris Arnold.

Left: Farmor's School moved into new buildings, built for 350 pupils, on 3 October 1961 and was officially opened on 16 February 1962. The school badge was taken from Elizabeth Farmor's coat of arms.

Built on the site of the old mansion, Park House, home of Elizabeth Farmor, this aerial view shows a number of temporary classroom blocks surrounding the main building to accommodate the ever increasing number of pupils. The school became comprehensive in 1966 and has been ranked in the top ten for exam results in the country. In 2007 there are over 1,000 pupils aged eleven to eighteen on roll, under the headship of Mrs Anne Stokes, making history as the first female head teacher in the school's long history.

Making it into the record books, too, fourteen sets of twins at Farmor's in 1987, shown here in their pairs for *The Times* photographer.

Left to right: Mandy and Tina Palmer, Katie and Joanna Lardner, Stephen and Robert Peyman, Paul and David Freebury, Matthew and Lea Payne, Rebecca and Gavin Landless, Jonathan and Edward Beachey, Alistair and Iain Ross, Anthony and Roger Pettifer, Iain and Helen Godfrey, Robin and Colin Hicks, Marie and Debbie Walden, Matthew and William Bloomer, Peter and Louise Naudi.

Christine Patheyjohns and Celia Gaiger – the model of concentration in the typewriting class in 1966.

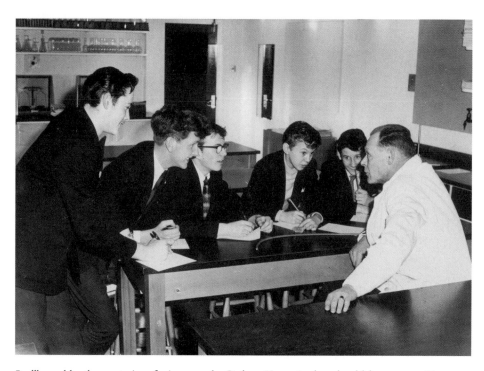

Spellbound by the mysteries of science under Robert Henry in the school laboratory, 1966.

Fifth-year football team, June 1977.

School Orchestra with Head of Music, Ted Mason, June 1977.

Oliver! The school's first major musical, directed by Harry Bilbrough as Fagin, Roger Bond, musical director and Maud Bond as Nancy, Hugh Dudley as Bill Sykes and Michael Carpenter as Oliver, 1971.

A motley crowd of artful dodgers with June Lewis as Mrs Bumble.

John Hartley as Mr Bumble on the left, Clive Watson as Mr Sowerberry, the undertaker, on the extreme right.

Fairford Primary School, under the headship of Frank Dipper (his daughter Jill is centre left of second row) with Class I in 1957, which included a number of Polish boys from the Polish Camp in Fairford Park (at the back of the picture). The new primary school, built opposite the Victorian infants' school, opened in 1954, taking 104 primary-age children from Farmor's junior section.

Mr Dipper, with teachers Sylvia Griffiths and Marion Chudley in 1975, with Gearings (once one of Fairford's home bakeries) in the background. The Orchard housing development now fills the former playing field.

The last day in the old primary school.

Part of the primary school can be seen over the top of the wall on the right as mothers wait for their children to leave the infants' school, which generations had attended since it was built in 1873. Much of the stone used in its construction was taken from the old workhouse that had stood in the Croft since 1773.

The lollipop lady on duty for the last time in London Street. The old infants' school now forms the children's section of the new library.

Above: Cutting the first sod of soil in the park for the site of the new primary school.

Below: September 1987: the new school opened in Leafield Road at the entrance to Farmor's School.

The overgrown riverside area leading from Waterloo Lane to Dilly's Bridge has been adopted as a community project by Coln House School.

Anthony Little, who spearheads the whole project, teaching in the open air classroom which the river bank has become for the lessons in pruning and scrub clearance.

After many months of hours of hard work, the pupils can now 'see the wood from the trees' with Dilly's Bridge leading off to the left in the background.

Spring 2007: with the tangled undergrowth cleared the plans that the pupils have worked on start to take shape.

So successful is the Coln House riverside project that Fairford and other neighbouring primary schools are getting involved in a wide range of environmental studies – and creating a rural haven to the benefit of the community of Fairford.

eight

Events

PROGRAMME OF
Fairford Carnival and Fete,
JULY 15th, 1920.

2 o'clock p.m.

PROCESSION will start from the Park and parade the Town, falling out in the Market Place.

3 and 6.30 o'clock.

STAGE PERFORMANCES

By the following London Star Artistes:

P. J. DURNEY, The World's Champion Rolling Globe Walker.
THREE FLYING FOXES, Aerial Gymnastics.
THE DERONEYS, Wire Walkers, &c., &c.
THE THREE ROLANDS, Balancers and Acrobats.
WILL DENVER, Eccentric Musical Comedian.
JACK WYMAN, The Great Australian Trick Skater.

4.30 o'clock.

Motor Car Gymkhana Sports.

From 4.30 to 6.30.

The PARK GARDENS will be open.

Admission 6d.   (Proceeds for the Fairford Hospital.)

4.45 and 7 o'clock.

Mr. J. B. Chesterman's Concert Party.

TEAS will be provided in the Park as usual.
(Arrangements will be made for adequate supplies.)

DANCING from 8 till 10.30 o'clock.

Fairford Carnival began in 1894 as a Cycle Carnival to raise funds for the Cottage Hospital to become billed as 'the best in the west' and, as seen in this programme of 1920, attracting star artistes from London to perform in the arena events.

Contemporary situations and national news were always portrayed in tableau on the horse-drawn floats.

The capture of a German gun from the First World War formed a genuine reminder of a peace that had been hard won a mere two years before this entry in 1920.

Above: The spectacular wedding cake entry by H.M. Powells, Drapers, won champion prize in 1935.

Left: As motor vehicles came in use alongside the horse and wagon, ingenious designs were created to maximum effect, such as this crinoline lady gliding along on a car.

Here, not only was a house created on wheels, but its greenhouse, too. All decorations were painstakingly made by hand using crêpe paper.

A local newspaper report on this entry of 1901 stated that 'it bore a striking resemblance to a baked potato engine', with the message hitting at the unsuccessful railway undertaking by the East Glos Railway Co. to link Fairford with Cirencester, 'the failure of which still rankles in the hearts of local people'!

The tea ladies under the direction of Mrs Gantlett, advertising in the 1939 programme *The Popular Tea Enclosure* where some 4,000 teas were served each year at a cost of 1s a family. A whole page advertisement in the same programme announced that the *First Class Tea Enclosure* was under the direction of Mrs Palmer (of Park House) and Lady Hirtzel as 1s 6d a head, children 1s each at 'tables shaded by beautiful trees and adjacent to the Band Enclosure'.

The newly formed Girl Guides company displayed their banner in the carnival of 1918.

Boy Scouts heading what looks like a British Legion parade as some of the men seem to be wearing medals.

A reunion of the Girl Guides that had been under Mrs Walter Jones of Morgan Hall being photographed by her daughter, Ruth Ritter, who hosted the garden party in 1983, assisted by guide leaders Sonia McDermott and Julie Eddolls.

Fairford Traction Engine and Steam Rally has been firmly established in the events calendar and attracts thousands of enthusiasts to wallow in the age of steam.

Mark Cowley and Sue Yells have been stalwart supporters since their early days. Here they handle a Marshall agricultural engine built in 1919 which began its working life for H.R. Cole of Cirencester.

The rally really is a family affair with all the fun of the fair.

The Derby and Joan Entertainers Club tripping the boards in the Palmer Hall in the 1950s.

Television stars, Trevor Eve, Elizabeth Richardson and Joanna McCallum, with Hotchkiss, the dog, on set in the High Street in 1986, which appeared as Abingford in 1947 in the film *A Wreath of Roses*.

Painting by Frank Baston, who, like most of Morgan Hall Artists' Cricket Club, formed by the famous American artist, Edwin Abbey, was a Royal Academician. Morgan Hall, where Abbey had the largest studio in England in the early 1900s, can be glimpsed in the background. The painting hangs in the Long Room at Trent Bridge.

Fairford cricketers in festive form for a match during the celebrations of their centenary at Park Street ground in 1989.

In the bleak midwinter, the 'waits' carol-singing outside St Mary's church before they appeared on stage inside for *A Christmas Carol* in 1990.

The ancient mummers' play brought to life in the 1980s. Left to right: Angela Yells, Samantha Jones, Sue Yells, Peter Yells, June Lewis, Peter Lidgard, Jenny Lidgard, Meg Perry and Paul Jones with Maurice Jones (as Belzebub) on the floor.

PRODUCTION

SCRIPTWRITER:	June R. Lewis	
MUSIC:	Director	– John Henderson, conductor and organist
		Fairford Church Choir
		Fairford Choral Society
		John Chudley (Tenor) Linda Cockins (Soprano)
		Emma Gayler (Solo)
		Gramophone records by permission
SOUND:	Director	– David Gayler
		Graham Partington, Alan Halfacre
		Murdock Fraser, Rupert Kirkham
LIGHTING:	Director	– David Williams
		Simon Tailford, Catherine Toomer
		William Somers, Alistair Ritchie
	with wiring assistants:	Peter Yells, Mark Westcott,
		Allan Gammond
PRODUCER:		Madeline Teed
	Assistants:	June Lewis
		Jocelyn Barker, Benedicta Nesham
STAGE STAFF MANAGER:		Don Cobbett
PROPS:		Muriel Matthewman, Mona Frow
		Mary Woolley, Unicorn Theatre Trust
STAGING:		Peter Yells, Geoffrey Teed
STAGE STAFF:		Barbara Cobbett, Joanna Cobbett,
		Stephanie Edwards, Margaret Fraser,
		Toby Keene, Anne Saunders,
		Fiona Paton, Carol Thompson
		Stephen Yells
PROMPT:		Diana Lee-Browne

The first major drama to be staged in St Mary's was a community project portraying over 1,000 years of history of the town in a *Son et Lumière* in 1978, and raised enough money to fund the building and financing of day hospital facilities at the Cottage Hospital.

Just a handful of the characters involved: Chris Harrison as Shepherd, Sid Jacques as Kimber the church verger, Jan Peters as Elizabeth of York, Geoffrey Teed as Steward to Henry VII, Liz Hope as Mrs Cowley with June Lewis, Shepherd Boy showing the script to Mark Cowley who played the part of an ancestral member of the family, the Revd Abraham Cowley.

Don Cobbett firmly directing every move, with Margaret Fraser and Carol Thompson, stage staff, concentrating at rehearsal.

Colin Watkins, headmaster of Fairford Primary School, rehearsing his pupils for their scene in which they all enacted school as it would have been in Victorian times, watched by Madeline Teed the producer.

Even the Cotswold sheep had to be shampooed before their star performance, certainly making history as the first sheep to be taken inside St Mary's – built on the profits of the medieval wool trade.

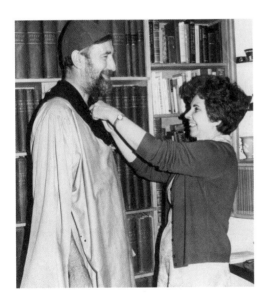

Above left: Liz Weeks, wardrobe mistress, sizing up Derrick Youngs as a medieval priest.

Above right: Keith Youngs, jester to Henry VIII. It was during his visit to Fairford for a week in 1520 that Henry VIII dubbed John Tame's grandson as Sir Edmond, made a special coat of arms of the supporters of the royal arms of England to the Tame family and appointed Sir Edmond, 'steward for life of the lordship of Fairford with xls a yeare'.

Charles I sampling the local fish and chips - Alan Baker caught behind the scenes!

Above left: Frank Hall made an impressive William the Conqueror.

Above right: United off stage, the opposing figures in the Civil War of Capt. Somerville, played by Michael Bottomley, and Col. Morgan, played by Ivor Price.

Playing themselves as angelic choirboys, Howard Price, James Cobbett and Stephen Price, looking as though butter wouldn't melt in their mouth – but the apples (in the Lady Chapel designed for props) were a different matter!

Dining formal style in the Palmer Hall, which was built for the town by Col. Palmer to commemorate the Silver Jubilee of George V in 1935, townsfolk celebrate the coronation of George VI in 1937.

Above: Eagerly awaiting their taste of the Coronation ox roast at Morgan Hall.

Below: Just to prove that interest in history can be fun, memories of former schooldays were recalled and re-enacted at Fairford History Society's school-dinners day held in the old Farmor's School: Colin Watkins, Ronald Taylor, Ralph Jones, Phil Hope, Ellis Hoult and Martin Harwood.

A gaggle of giggling 'schoolgirls': June Lewis-Jones, Liz Taylor, Jeanne Watkins, Liz Hope, Diana Routledge, Terry Hoult, Chris Roberts and Jane Hawkes.

Trevor Hing, Alison Hobson and Pamela Nelmes ready to serve up the traditional school dinner: shepherd's pie and rice pudding with jam.

True to form, someone 'is given lines': Ralph Jones copies out 'I must respect my Headmaster', watched by John Hunt, Phil and Liz Hope and Martin Harwood.

Fairford really goes to town when it gathers together to celebrate national events. Here, the patriotic theme procession filled the long High Street for Queen Elizabeth II's Silver Jubilee in 1977.

Martin Lee-Browne enjoying the pram race, pushed by John Malleson.

Twenty-five years later, Fairford gets in good voice to celebrate the Queen's Golden Jubilee, led here by Jean and Barry Kilgariff.

Oyez! Maurice Jones in full cry leading the procession.

Getting ready for the children's party in the Market Place, and making memories again of another national milestone as celebrated local style.

nine

In War and Peace

Above: Fairford Platoon Home Guard, assembled outside the Congregational chapel in the Croft in 1943 where they had their headquarters.

Below: A few of the 'Mum's Army' who cooked meals for the evacuees at The Settlement in Park Street under the auspices of the WVS.

Some of the 151 schoolchildren, mainly from the Barking, Holborn and West Ham districts who were evacuated to Fairford, along with their teachers – outnumbering the entire number of children on roll at Farmor's at the time.

The evacuees were registered separately from the local children, showing their destination when they left Farmor's; a handful of families remained and made Fairford their home after the war.

Wallace J. Glavor was stationed at 186th USAF General Hospital and 'liberated' the town's Union Jack during the VE celebrations, taking it back to the States as a souvenir of Fairford. He returned it to the town some fifty-three years later!

Above: One of the many evacuees at The Settlement, that had been furnished and equipped by local people, painted by Rosemary Gwynne-Jones who was the official war artist for the Fairford centre.

Opposite above: RAF Fairford Base at the foot of Horcott Hill was constructed specifically in readiness of the invasion of Europe. The Base opened on 18 January 1944 under Number 38 Transport Command of the RAF and in March fifty Stirling IV aircraft and 100 Horsa gliders arrived, followed by the crews of 620 and 190 Squadrons. This page from Pilot Cyril Shuttlewood's log book shows the 18 September 1944 entry for Operation Market (the code name for the Arnhem landing). The 190 Squadron suffered the loss of ten of the fourteen aircraft shot down from Fairford.

YEAR 1944 MONTH	DATE	AIRCRAFT Type	No.	PILOT, OR 1ST PILOT	2ND PILOT, PUPIL OR PASSENGER	DUTY (INCLUDING RESULTS AND REMARKS)	SINGLE-ENGINE AIRCRAFT DAY Dual (1)	Pilot (2)	NIGHT Dual (3)	Pilot (4)	MULTI-ENGINE AIRCRAFT DAY Dual (5)	1st Pilot (6)	2nd Pilot (7)	NIGHT Dual (8)	1st Pilot (9)	2nd Pilot (10)	PASS-ENGER (11)	INSTR/CLOUD FLYING [Incl. in cols. (1) to (10)] Dual (12)	Pilot (13)
—	—	—	—	—	—	TOTALS BROUGHT FORWARD	41·35	82·05	6·15	4·05	14·15	130·10	22·45	1·55	6·05		64·10	7·10	50·3
SEP.	11	HORSA	LG918	SELF	SGT. JOHNSON SGT. HATCH (4 PASSENGERS)	6,000' RELEASE						·20							
SEP.	18	HORSA	DP532	SELF	SGT. JOHNSON	OPERATION MARKET—(ARNHEM) JEEP, 2 TRAILERS, 2 m/c's, 2 TROOPS						3·30							·1
					A/c TYPES HORSA	SUMMARY FOR SEP. 1944 UNIT - 'G' SQDN. DATE - 15 OCT. 1944 SIGNATURE - R. Littlewood						3·50							·1
OCT.	22	HORSA	DP525	SELF	SGT. JOHNSON SGT. WILLCOX	FULL LOAD - FAIRFORD TO GT. DUNMOW						·45							·1
OCT.	30	HORSA	LH340	SELF (SAFETY	SGT. JOHNSON	EXERCISE ESSEX - LIGHT LOAD.						2·00							·10
OCT.	31	HORSA	RW771	SELF	PILOT) SGT. CROSSLAND	LOCAL CROSS-COUNTRY						·30							
					A/c TYPES HORSA	SUMMARY FOR OCT. 1944 UNIT - 'G' SQDN. DATE - 5 NOV. 1944 SIGNATURE - R. Littlewood						3·15							·10
				GRAND TOTAL [Cols. (1) to (10)] 316 Hrs. 15 Mins.		TOTALS CARRIED FORWARD	41·35	82·05	6·5	4·05	14·5	137·05	22·45	1·55	6·05		64·10	7·10	1·00

Below: This tranquil spot on a small plateau on the rise of ground just beyond the gardens of Totterdown Farmhouse was the site of 'The Cage', set up as a strictly secure tented centre which was completely surrounded by double barbed wire, where sections of the SAS were held during their training. Set up on the perimeter of the RAF Base in May 1944 in readiness for their participation in the Second Front, the SAS were dropped in 'sticks' of four to thirty at a time. Sometimes expected by the French Underground Movement (the Maquis), other times the men went 'blind' and had to sort themselves out on the ground in enemy held territory. In later missions, jeeps were dropped to give the units the necessary mobility and fire power. *These men are dangerous*, the title of Derrick Harrison's book, recorded just how courageous and vital their role was in the war.

Above: Vera Noden at the age of nineteen was the youngest NAAFI girl at The Cage catering for the SAS in makeshift conditions. The six women and a male manager, who ran the NAAFI were 'sealed' in The Cage with the men of the SAS during the long periods of their briefing and secret service training from which they left for their dangerous missions by way of the Totterdown Farm track. But even under those austere conditions romance bloomed, and Vera met her future husband Sgt 'Darkie' Chappell at The Cage at Fairford.

Opposite above: Fairford Park was requisitioned for military use during the war. The 186th General Hospital USA was built in the old Deer Park, north of the mansion house. The old war-time hospital buildings were utilised after the war as a settlement camp for displaced Polish families. In 1949 some 1,200 Poles lived at Fairford Polish Hostel, which survived for another decade before the camp was dispersed and the families moved to other communities – mainly in the Swindon area. Edward Czopek, front left, stayed and made Fairford his home.

Below left: One of the Poles who served under General Anders in Italy, returning from work to his family at Fairford Polish Hostel.

Below right: Edward's tombstone which says it all: it is also unusual to have a Polish grave in the churchyard of St Mary's, most are to be found at the Roman Catholic church at Horcott.

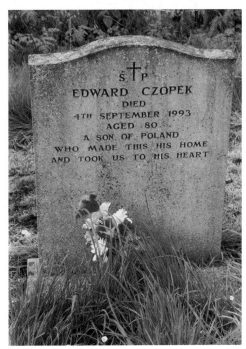

Above: One of the star attractions in 1993 was the appearance of the first Russian plane on British soil, the great Tupelov Bear. In the background (above the tail) can be seen the famous Red Arrows aerobatic team which was also based for many years in the Cotswolds.

Opposite above: The first aeroplane to be seen close to by most people in Fairford by about 1920 was this one – thought to be an RE 8 of the First World War – that crash landed in a field alongside the Southrop Road.

Opposite below: South Hill farm house, built in the Georgian style for Capt Rickards in 1928 at a cost of £35,000, which was deemed by the Air Ministry to be too high by 23ft as it was in the approach path of the proposed extension to RAF Base runway. This photograph was taken in 1938. The family had to move out in 1952 and the house was demolished. The Base was extended even further when it became the BAC test centre for Concorde in the 1970s. A memorial seat in the grounds of the town library is to Brian Trubshaw, who flew Concorde into Fairford on its maiden flight on 9 April 1969.

Left: Aircraft from all corners of the globe now come to RAF Fairford Base every July to the Royal International Air Tattoo, attracting thousands of visitors to what is officially designated the greatest air show in the world.

Below: Back in the town, with their feet firmly on the ground, RAF Fairford's American schoolchildren add their Stars and Stripes to the Union Jack flags in this procession celebrating the Queen's Golden Jubilee.

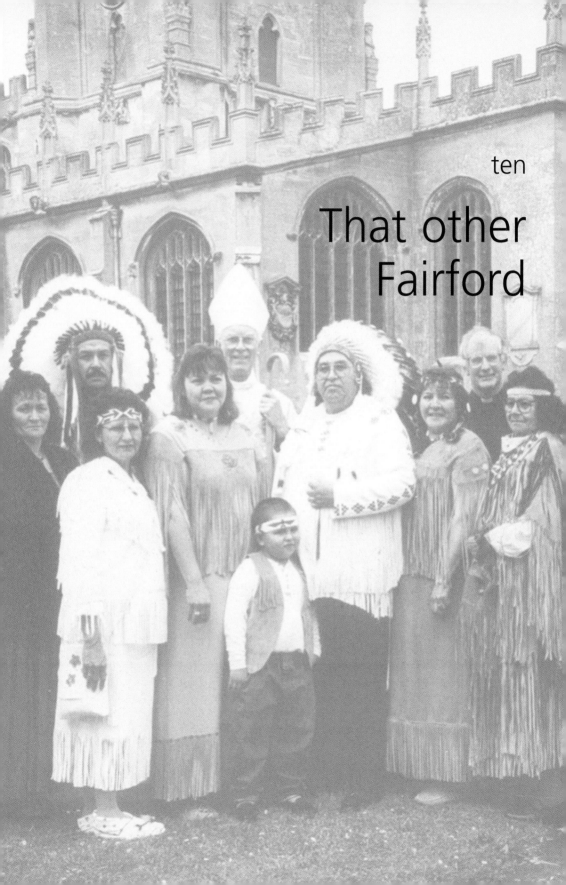

ten

That other Fairford

Left: Welcome to Pinn Nay Moo Ta – that other Fairford: an Indian Reservation in the Interlake section between the great prairies and the 100,000 lakes of Manitoba.

Above left: Archdeacon Abraham Cowley who went as a young twenty-five-year-old Anglican missionary to Rupert's Land in North America in 1841. Abraham Cowley was the son of a stone mason of this Fairford and, influenced by the Revd Francis Rice (who later became Lord Dynevor), joined the Church Missionary Society.

Above right: Led by a handful of native Indians, Abraham Cowley eventually made his way by canoe into the great river that flows between Lake Manitoba and Lake Winnipeg and came across a small band of eleven families of Ojibwa Saulteaux Indians camped on the wooded bank for the spring fishing during a lull in their constant warring with the Crees. Cowley was the first white man the Indians had ever seen and was saved from capture by the fact that their wise men had told them that one day they would be visited by the 'great white spirit'. After much hard and dedicated work, Cowley built a wooden church on the spot he had landed and a mission house with a small schoolroom. When the Archbishop of Rupert's Land and Primate of Canada visited the mission about 1890 he changed the Ojibwa name from Pinn Nay Moo Ta to Fairford in honour of the work done by Abraham Cowley.

The picture shows St Helen's church in winter when the temperature drops to minus 30 for at least four months. Also built of wood, this church replaced the one Cowley built further down river that eventually got washed away.

Above left: Chief Ke-Wee-tah-quun-ne-yash (he who flies round the feathers), the first elected Chief of Fairford Ojibwa Indians within the Swan Creek and Lake Manitoba area, wearing the Treaty medal. The long, unpronounceable native names defeated the recording officers so relevant Indians were dubbed with English names – hence Richard Woodhouse, who had constructed a 'wooden tent' as a more substantial dwelling for his family, following the building principles he learnt from Abraham Cowley.

Above right: The Treaty emblem which, among the assurances and promises made on 3 August 1871:

> *between Her Most Gracious Majesty the Queen of Great Britain and Ireland and the Chippewa and Swampy Cree Tribes and all other of the Indians inhabiting the district described the Indians hereby cede, release, surrender and yield up to Her Majesty and successors for ever all the lands specified … for as long as the sun shines the rivers flow and grass grows ….*

Among the regulations were:

> *no intoxicating liquor to be introduced or sold on the Reservation, and 'from Her majesty's bounty and benevolence each Chief who signed the Treaty, a dress distinguishing him as Chief, for braves and for councillors of each Chief a dress and for each, except Yellow Quill, a buggy, a bull and a cow, with a boar for each Reserve, and a sow for each Chief….*

Abraham Cowley was one of the witnesses at the signing of the Treaty and it is interesting that of all the chiefs of the other tribes who 'signed' by 'making their cross', only Richard Woodhouse of Fairford was able to write his name.

A message of goodwill from Canadian Fairford to English Fairford in 1978 with the traditional Ojibwa beaded and feathered breastplate made by Kathleen Baer to be worn in this Fairford's *Son et Lumière*, in which David Pitts played the part of an Indian converted by Abraham Cowley in a scene telling the story of that other Fairford.

Opposite above: The heads of the respective Fairfords met when some twenty-six Fairford Indians came to our English Fairford to commemorate the 500th anniversary of the consecration of St Mary's church in 1997. Fairford Town Mayor, Freda Lang, wears her chain of office with the badge of the Tame coat of arms as she greets Chief Ed Anderson, wearing his ceremonial headdress.

Opposite middle: Lining up for the television cameras, an impressive procession from the Market Place, St Mary's church choir led by the town crier, followed by mounties, chiefs and clergy under the watchful eye of this Fairford's vicar, the Revd John Willard on the left with Father Ron MacCullough of Canadian Fairford in the background.

Opposite below: A truly historic occasion: the Bishop of Gloucester and the Revd John Willard outside St Mary's church from where Abraham Cowley left on his mission in 1841. Among the Ojibwa Saulteaux Indians are the present Chief, two former chiefs, the Medicine Woman and two mounties – all of whom were born and live in 'that other Fairford' some 4,500 miles apart.

Other local titles published by Tempus

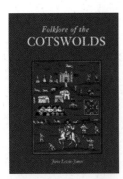

Folklore of the Cotswolds

JUNE LEWIS-JONES

This detailed book by folklore enthusiast June Lewis-Jones, explores the heritage of folklore that has always been so prevalent throughout the Cotswolds, from cures and remedies, recipes and traditions to dance, song, music and mumming. It includes mysteries, tales of witches and ghosts, legends born of the landscape, such as the Devil's Chimney and the Rollright Stones, and lesser-known Cotswold stories like the secret marriage at Snowshill Manor.

978 07524 2930 2

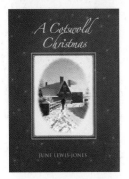

Cotswold Christmas

JUNE LEWIS-JONES

Explore the rich heritage of Christmas past in the Cotswolds with this varied collection of carols and customs, seasonal recipes and stories, pastimes, poetry, folklore and reminiscences. From Morris dancing and wassailing to Mrs Beeton's recipe for the perfect Christmas dinner, this enthralling collection will be a welcome addition to any anthology of the county and a seasonal treat for all.

978 07524 3975 4

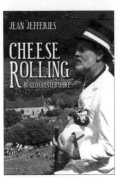

Cheese Rolling in Gloucestershire

JEAN JEFFERIES

Each year on May Bank Holiday Monday, guest 'rollers' hurl 7lb Double Gloucester cheeses down the precariously steep Coopers Hill in Gloucestershire whilst a bunch of reckless competitors chase after them. The aim of each of the four races is to be the first to cross the winning line at the foot of the hill and win the cheese. This fascinating book covers every possible aspect of Coopers' Hill Cheese Rolling traditions both past and present, and is illustrated with over 200 images.

978 07524 4302 7

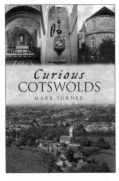

Curious Cotswolds

MARK TURNER

In common with many parts of Britain, the Cotswolds has an abundance of curiosities. For those who are perennially attracted to anything that might be termed 'curious' – an ancient standing stone, a little-known beauty spot, a disused aerodrome, a folly erected by some eccentric egotist, or perhaps the site of an unsolved murder – this book will satisfy even the most ardent enthusiast by uncovering some f the area's most fascinating people, places and events.

978 07524 3930 3

If you are interested in purchasing other books published by Tempus, or in case you have difficulty finding any Tempus books in your local bookshop, you can also place orders directly through our website

www.tempus-publishing.com